DIM SUM MADE EASY

DIM SUM

MADE EASY

Lucille Liang

Sterling Publishing Co., Inc.
New York

Library of Congress Cataloging-in-Publication Data

Liang, Lucille.
  Dim sum made easy / Lucille Liang.
       p. cm.
  Includes index.
  ISBN-13: 978-1-4027-2008-6
  ISBN-10: 1-4027-2008-4
  1. Dim sum. 2. Snack foods--China. 3. Cookery, Chinese. I. Title.

TX773.L4827 2006
641.5951—dc22

                                                          2005037592

              2 4 6 8 10 9 7 5 3 1

                 The material in this book has been adapted from:
                Chinese Regional Cooking © 2002 by Lucille Liang

       Every effort has been made to ensure that all the information in this book is accurate.
       However, due to differing conditions, tools, and individual skills, the publisher cannot
                    be responsible for any injuries, losses, and/or damages
                     which may result from the use of information in this book.

                      Published by Sterling Publishing Co., Inc.
                     387 Park Avenue South, New York, NY 10016

                          © 2006 by Sterling Publishing Co., Inc.

                      Distributed in Canada by Sterling Publishing
                  c/o Canadian Manda Group, 165 Dufferin Street
                           Toronto, Ontario, Canada M6K 3H6
                   Distributed in the United Kingdom by GMC Distribution Services
                  Castle Place, 166 High Street, Lewes, East Sussex, England BN7 1XU
                   Distributed in Australia by Capricorn Link (Australia) Pty. Ltd.
                           P.O. Box 704, Windsor, NSW 2756, Australia

                                Printed in China

CONTENTS

INTRODUCTION TO DIM SUM

Dim sum, a Cantonese term, means "heart's delight"—signifying small foods that delight one's heart. Traditionally, dim sum are foods served in small portions, so that the diner can sample a wide variety of dishes. A dim sum plate typically has about four bite-size portions of a dish, with many different plates presented during the dim sum meal. In China, dim sum is usually a morning or early afternoon treat, taken with tea. Here in the U.S., the term has evolved to broadly refer to a meal or snack consisting of many varieties of bite-size foods served at any time of the day. And because of their bite-size nature, many dim sum dishes make wonderful appetizer or hors d'oeuvres to start a Western meal.

In a traditional dim sum restaurant, servers push carts filled with plates past diners, who ask for a plate when they see an appealing dish. Served in this manner, dim sum dishes arrive throughout a meal rather than all at once.

Most of the recipes in this book are for traditional dim sum dishes—dumplings, pork buns, shrimp balls, etc. But also included are other Chinese dishes that are not usually considered dim sum but can be easily served dim-sum style. To serve an appetizer or side dish in dim-sum fashion, divide the food into bite-size portions and place three to four portions per plate. The food can also be served buffet-style, where diners can help themselves to small portions.

A FEW NOTES ABOUT THE RECIPES

The recipes in *Dim Sum Made Easy* use authentic Chinese ingredients—for instance, Chinese rice wine (instead of dry sherry), and tapioca starch (instead of cornstarch). It is these authentic ingredients that make the dishes taste truly Chinese. If at all possible, seek out these ingredients—they will make a difference in your final dish. For example, tapioca starch is lighter than cornstarch and gives a lighter, crisper texture; and when used as a thickening agent, it adds an attractive glaze that cornstarch does not. Descriptions of ingredients that may be unfamiliar to you—such as red-in-snow, canned quail eggs, spicy rice powder—are at the end of the respective recipe.

If you would like to double or triple a recipe, generally you will need to double or triple every ingredient accordingly. However, you usually do not need to double the oil; you can use less. For instance, if 2 tablespoons of oil is called for in a recipe, when you double the recipe you do not need to use $1/4$ cup of oil; 3 tablespoons will probably be sufficient. For those on a low-sodium diet, the amount of salt need not be doubled strictly.

Keep in mind that with all quantities of seasonings, the measurements are only recommendations to suit general tastes; you may decide you like more or less salt, sugar, seasonings, and so forth.

Everything in this book will work successfully if you follow the recipes carefully. But do read the recipes through several times before you attempt to prepare them. Furthermore, do not try a recipe for the first time at a dinner party. Always "try out" a recipe for the family before making it for company.

CHINESE COOKING UTENSILS

Proper Chinese cooking utensils not only make cooking easier, they also impart confidence in the cook—and they can be a lot of fun to use! The following are some of the basic utensils that no Chinese cook would consider his kitchen equipment complete without:

A **WOK** is the most ingenious and versatile cooking utensil. Since it is roomy and round-bottomed, food can be tossed and stirred easily in it. It is used extensively for stir-frying and steaming. In addition, it's the perfect vessel for frying or scrambling eggs.

The best wok is one of heavy-duty carbon steel, and the most practical size has a 14-inch (35-cm) diameter. (Experts usually do not recommend stainless steel, aluminum, or electric woks.) A wok with a long wooden handle is handy since you can hold the handle while stir-frying without risk of burning your hand. If you have an electric stove, a flat-bottomed wok is best because a large surface area touches the burner, creating more efficient heating. If you have a gas stove, a round-bottomed wok (with a metal ring to stabilize it) is your best bet.

It is important to season a new wok before using it, to prevent food from sticking and the metal from rusting. To season a wok: Wash off the mechanical oil both inside and out with hot water and detergent and wipe the wok dry. Then coat the entire interior surface of the wok with a little vegetable oil; heat the oil on medium heat for 1 minute, while tilting and rotating the wok; wipe off the oil with a paper towel. Repeat this process (coat with oil, heat over medium heat, and wipe with paper towel). Now the wok is ready to be used. A wok that is well-seasoned by constant use will never rust. But if you do not use it often, you should coat the wok with a little oil before storage. After the wok has been seasoned, do not use detergent to wash it. Just scrub the wok with a hard brush under hot running water. The best way to dry the wok is to place it on the stove over medium heat for several minutes until it is completely dry.

A **CLEAVER** is indispensable in Chinese cooking. See Basic Cutting Techniques (page 11) for the uses of a cleaver and methods of cutting.

A **STEAMER** is equally important in Chinese cooking, since steaming is one of the major cooking methods. Two kinds of steamers are available: bamboo and aluminum. A bamboo steamer, used in a wok, ventilates well and, since it is a beautiful utensil, dishes can be served directly from the steamer. An aluminum steamer set, not quite as pretty as a bamboo steamer, includes a bottom pot to hold water and so does not need to be set in a wok.

Before its first use, a new bamboo steamer should be placed over boiling water in a wok for one hour to remove the bamboo smell. Whenever you are steaming for a long period of time, a pot of boiling water should be kept ready to add to the wok as necessary.

Chinese **SPATULAS, LADLES, CHOPSTICKS, WIRE SIEVES,** and a good **CHOPPING BOARD** are also important in making the cooking easier and more enjoyable.

CHINESE COOKING METHODS

Methods for cooking dim sum are as varied as the types of dim sum. Steaming, stir-frying, deep-frying, red-cooking—all are used when making succulent dim sum dishes.

STEAMING

Steaming is a frequent dim sum cooking method and steamers are important cooking utensils in China. To steam, you can use a steamer set, a contraption similar to a double boiler with a container on top for the food and a pan underneath for boiling water. You can also steam with a bamboo steamer which is set over boiling water in a large wok. Either way, the intense steam from boiling water circulates and cooks the food, intensifying the taste of well-seasoned food. Steaming is also a healthful way of cooking since oil is not usually used. Steamed Pearl Balls (page 41), Spareribs Steamed with Spicy Rice Powder (page 63), and many dumplings (pages 22, 29, and 31) are some of the recipes here that incorporate steaming.

DEEP-FRYING

Deep-frying is a process shared by many cuisines—but it is especially popular when making Chinese dim sum. In deep-frying, food is submerged in a large amount of hot oil until golden brown and thoroughly cooked. Shrimp Laver Rolls (page 33), Shanghai Spring Rolls (page 34), Deep-Fried Shrimp Balls (page 39), and Fish Wrapped in Tofu Skin (page 44) are examples of the deep-fried dim sum treats here. Sometimes deep-frying is used as a preparatory step—such as with Quail Eggs in Brown Sauce (page 49), where the quail eggs are deep-fried before being stir-fried with vegetables.

SHALLOW-FRYING

Shallow-frying is similar to French sautéing. Food is browned slowly in hot oil over medium heat for several minutes and then turned over to brown the other side. This method is often used for food that has already been partially cooked, such as Chinese Fried Noodles, Both Sides Brown (page 17).

STIR-FRYING

Stir-frying is very popular in Chinese cooking: Meat and vegetable stir-fries served over rice are a staple of home and restaurant cooking. When making dim sum, stir-frying is usually used as a preliminary or intermediate step—to cook and combine fillings for Spring Rolls (page 34) or to make Stir-Fried Rice Cakes (page 70). To stir-fry means that small pieces of food are tossed and turned continuously over high heat in a small amount of oil for a short period of time. Since most ingredients are cut into bite-size pieces before stir-frying, the cooking time is short, fuel is saved, and nutritious vitamins and minerals are preserved.

RED-COOKING

In red-cooking, or Chinese stewing, food is simmered slowly in dark soy sauce, which gives it a deep reddish color. Star anise, five-spice powder, ginger, and scallions are often used to give the dish a distinctive aroma, and rice wine and rock sugar are used for mellow taste and a glazed sauce. Spiced Pork (page 57) and Sweet and Sour Spareribs (page 59) exemplify this type of cooking. An advantage of the red-cooking method is that the dish can be cooked in advance and reheated before serving; the flavor often intensifies in reheating.

CHINESE CUTTING TECHNIQUES

In Chinese cooking, most ingredients are cut into uniform bite-size or smaller pieces before cooking. Therefore, learning how to slice and chop efficiently is important.

One of the indispensable utensils of the cook is a cleaver. Without a cleaver, a cook would need a great variety of knives to do the different jobs required in Chinese cooking. The cleaver provides both weight, important for chopping and mincing, and dexterity, essential to thin slicing and fine shredding. All parts of the cleaver are useful. The sharp edge of the cleaver is used to slice, shred, dice, mince, and chop. The blunt edge of the cleaver is used to tenderize meat by pounding the meat and to crush items like ginger and garlic. The wooden handle also has its use—to grind or pound ingredients into powder form. In addition, after cutting, one can use the flat side of the cleaver as a spatula to lift the cut pieces into a dish. Chinese cleavers come in different weights and sizes, but the best choice is a number 3 or 4 carbon-steel cleaver, which is used to cut both meat and vegetables.

To cut with the cleaver, place the food on a chopping board. Hold the cleaver firmly with your right hand (if you are right-handed), with the thumb and forefinger falling on either side of the blade. With the left hand, hold and press in place the item to be cut, but make sure that your fingers are bent, clawlike, so that the first joints stick out—not your fingertips! This way you will not have any accidents because your fingertips are tucked away. Note that the cutting motion is not just an up-and-down motion; it is a forward and downward motion, with the strength coming from the shoulder.

Here are some basic ways of cutting:

SLICING

There are two kinds of slicing: straight and slant. Straight slicing is done with the cleaver perpendicular to the item to be sliced. The slices should generally be very thin. Slant slicing is done with the cleaver at a 45-degree angle to the food. This method of slicing is used whenever you want to cut thin, wide slices from flat or small items.

SHREDDING

First cut the food into thin slices and then cut these slices into uniform shreds about 2 inches (5 cm) long. Several slices may be piled on top of one another before shredding.

DICING

First cut the food lengthwise into strips $1/4$ inch (6 mm) to $1/2$ inch (1.5 cm) wide, then cut these strips into small cubes or dice.

MINCING OR FINELY CHOPPING

First slice, then shred, and then cut the shreds into very fine pieces.

RECIPES

COLD NOODLES WITH SESAME SAUCE

Cold sesame noodles are popular picnic fare in China and perfect for other summertime meals. If serving as dim sum, combine all the ingredients and toss to combine before serving small individual servings. If you would like to serve larger portions, the pork, cucumbers, egg shreds, and cold noodles can be served in separate dishes so that each diner can create a salad according to individual taste. Makes about 16 dim sum servings.

1 pound (500 g) fresh egg noodles

2 tablespoons sesame oil

1 tablespoon dark soy sauce

2 eggs

pinch of salt

1 tablespoon peanut or vegetable oil

SESAME SAUCE

2 tablespoons sesame seed paste, diluted with 3 tablespoons warm water

2 tablespoons dark soy sauce

2 cloves garlic, finely chopped

2 scallions, finely chopped

1 tablespoon white rice vinegar

2 teaspoons sugar

2 teaspoons hot oil (chili oil)

$1/2$ teaspoon salt

1 cucumber, peeled, seeded, and shredded

$1/2$ pound (250 g) roast pork, cut into 2-inch (5-cm) strips

1.   Cook the noodles in a large pot of boiling water 4 to 5 minutes. Rinse under cold water and drain thoroughly. Add the sesame oil and soy sauce to the noodles and toss well. Cover and refrigerate until ready to serve.

2.   Beat the eggs with the salt and set aside for 10 minutes. Heat a scant teaspoon oil in a wok over medium-high heat. Pour in one-fourth of the beaten egg and make an egg sheet by swirling egg onto sides of wok. Lift up and flip over and let cook briefly on the other side. Repeat to make 3 more sheets. Let the egg sheets cool. Shred into 2-inch-long (5-cm-long) strips. Set aside.

3.   To make the Sesame Sauce: Mix the sesame seed paste, soy sauce, garlic, scallions, vinegar, sugar, hot oil, and salt in a small bowl.

4.   When it is time to serve, add the sauce to the noodles and toss well. Transfer the noodles to a large platter. Top with the egg strips, shredded cucumber, and roast pork and toss to mix.

VARIATIONS Shredded cold chicken can used instead of roast pork. You can also substitute bean sprouts and shredded Chinese cabbage for the cucumbers.

Chinese Fried Noodles, Both Sides Brown

"Both sides brown" is a fancy way to serve noodles and this dish is considered quite a treat. Boiled noodles are first shallow-fried until crunchy and golden brown on both sides, then crowned with a glazed topping of stir-fried meat and vegetables. The noodles acquire flavors from the thickened sauce, but they are not soaked through. **Makes about 8 dim sum servings.**

PORK AND MARINADE
1 tablespoon light soy sauce
$1^1/_2$ teaspoons tapioca starch
1 teaspoon Chinese rice wine
$^1/_2$ pound (250 g) pork or beef, cut into 2-inch (5-cm) strips

6 to 8 dried Chinese mushrooms
$^1/_2$ pound (250 g) dried Canton noodles
9 tablespoons peanut or vegetable oil
2 tablespoons tapioca starch

$1^1/_2$ cups chicken broth
3 cups shredded Chinese cabbage
1 cup bamboo shoots, shredded
1 teaspoon salt

1. To make the marinade: Combine the soy sauce, tapioca starch, and rice wine in a large bowl. Add the pork or beef and marinate at least 30 minutes.

2. Soak the mushrooms in hot water until soft, 20 minutes; drain. Discard the stems. Shred the caps. Set aside. Soak the dried Canton noodles in boiling water 1 minute. Rinse with cold water and drain. Transfer to a medium bowl, add 2 tablespoons oil to prevent sticking, and set aside. Mix the tapioca starch with $^1/_2$ cup broth; set aside.

3. Heat 5 tablespoons of the remaining oil in a wok over medium-high heat until hot. Add the noodles and fry until the bottom is golden brown; turn the noodles over to brown the other side. Transfer the browned noodle cake to a warm platter and keep warm in a low oven while cooking the sauce.

4. Heat the remaining 2 tablespoons oil in the wok; stir in the meat and its marinade and stir-fry about 2 minutes. Add the shredded mushrooms, remaining 1 cup broth, cabbage, bamboo shoots, and salt. Cook over medium high heat until tender, stirring constantly. Stir in the tapioca starch mixture and cook, stirring, until thickened. Pour the sauce over the noodle cake and serve immediately.

DO AHEAD The noodles can be browned ahead of time and kept at room temperature. Just before serving, warm the noodles in a 375°F (182°C) oven while making the sauce in the wok.

VARIATION Chicken or shrimp can be used instead of pork or beef.

FRIED NOODLES AND CHICKEN WRAPPED IN LETTUCE LEAVES

In this fun dish, crunchy white cellophane noodles are mixed with colorful diced ham, chicken, vegetables, and egg, then wrapped with crispy lettuce leaves. The combination of flavors coupled with the crunchiness is what makes this dish special. **Makes about 20 dim sum servings.**

SEASONING SAUCE
2 tablespoons chicken broth

1 1/2 tablespoons light soy sauce

1 teaspoon sesame oil

1/2 teaspoon salt

1/8 teaspoon white or black pepper

CHICKEN AND MARINADE
1 tablespoon Chinese rice wine

1 tablespoon tapioca starch

1/2 teaspoon salt

1 skinned and boned whole chicken breast or chicken cutlet (about 1/4 pound or 125 g), cut into 1/4-inch (6-mm) dice

6 to 8 dried Chinese mushrooms

1/4 cup coarsely chopped Smithfield ham

1/2 cup green peas

2 eggs, beaten

2 ounces (60 g) cellophane noodles

1 cup plus 4 tablespoons peanut or vegetable oil

1 cup bamboo shoots, diced

20 lettuce leaves (nice, round pieces)

1. To make the Seasoning Sauce: Combine the broth, soy sauce, sesame oil, salt, and pepper in a small bowl. Set aside.

2. To make the marinade: Combine the rice wine, tapioca starch, and salt in a large bowl. Add the chicken and marinate at least 20 minutes. Soak the mushrooms in hot water until soft, 20 minutes; drain. Discard the stems. Dice the mushrooms into 1/4-inch (6-mm) pieces.

3. Boil the ham in a small pot of water 10 minutes; remove with a slotted spoon. When cool, cut into 1/4-inch (6-mm) dice. Boil the green peas in the boiling water for 1 minute. Drain and rinse with cold water.

4. Heat a wok over medium-high heat until very hot. Reduce the heat to low and allow the wok to cool 2 minutes. Pour in one-fourth of the beaten egg, swirl around the wok until a thin round egg sheet forms. Turn the sheet over and cook about 30 seconds more. Transfer to a plate and cool. Repeat 3 times with the remaining egg. When cool, cut the egg sheets into 1/4-inch (6-mm) pieces.

5. Cut and loosen the cellophane noodles and separate them into several batches. Heat 1 cup oil in the wok over medium-high heat until very hot. Deep-fry the cellophane noodles, a few at a time, until puffed up, just 2 or 3 seconds on each side. Transfer to a platter.

6. Discard the oil in the wok. Add 2 tablespoons fresh oil to the wok and heat over medium-high heat. Add the marinated diced chicken and stir-fry 30 seconds, or until it turns white. Drain and set aside.

7. Add 2 tablespoons oil to the wok and heat over medium-high heat. Add the diced ham, mushrooms, green peas, and bamboo shoots and stir-fry about 1 minute. Add the cooked chicken, diced egg, and seasoning sauce. Stir-fry over high heat until heated through and thoroughly mixed. Spoon the meat and vegetables over the cellophane noodles.

8. Diners should help themselves by putting some of the meat and noodle mixture in a lettuce leaf and wrapping the leaf around the mixture.

DO AHEAD The cellophane noodles can be deep-fried ahead of time and kept in a tightly covered jar or container. The meat and vegetables can be stir-fried and kept warm in the oven. Do not combine the two until you are ready to serve.

WONTONS

Simple but versatile, filling but not heavy, easy to cook and serve, wontons are a favorite food with the Chinese—as dim sum or in savory soups. For a bit richer flavor, fry the boiled wontons in a little bit of vegetable oil in a nonstick pan for a few minutes on each side; these crispy wontons will become your favorite dim sum. Serve with a dipping sauce (page 26 or 31), if you like. Or serve as an appetizer in chicken broth garnished with whole shrimp. **Makes about 60 wontons.**

1 package round wonton wrappers
  (60), thawed if frozen

FILLING
1 pound (500 g) ground pork

1 egg

3 tablespoons sesame oil

3 tablespoons dark soy sauce

1 tablespoon chicken broth

1 tablespoon Chinese rice wine

1 scallion, chopped

1 teaspoon chopped gingerroot

$^1/_2$ teaspoon salt

1.   Remove the wonton wrappers from the package and cover with wet towels for 15 minutes before use.

2.   To make the Filling: In a large bowl, combine the ground pork, egg, sesame oil, soy sauce, broth, rice wine, scallion, gingerroot, and salt.

3.   Place $^1/_2$ teaspoon filling in the center of one wrapper. Moisten the edge of the wrapper with some water and fold over at the center. Gently press the edges together. Fold in half again lengthwise and then pull the corners one over the other and press them together with a little water. (See illustrations at right.) A properly wrapped wonton resembles a nurse's cap. Repeat to make about 60 wontons.

4.   Bring 4 quarts of water to a boil in a deep pot or wok. Add the wontons to the boiling water and bring to a boil. Add 1 cup cold water and again bring to a boil. Repeat the process twice, each time adding 1 cup cold water and bringing the pot to a boil. When wontons float to the surface again, they are ready. Drain and serve.

DO AHEAD Wontons can be made weeks ahead of time and frozen before cooking. No need to defrost before cooking.

Steamed Shrimp Dumplings

These tasty dumplings, called *har gow*, are a Cantonese specialty and one of the most popular dim sum in China. Wheat starch makes the dough translucent and delicate, while the filling, tasty and crunchy, is accented by chopped shrimp and fresh water chestnuts. Wheat starch is a gluten-free flour found in Asian markets. Makes about 36 dumplings.

FILLING

1 pound (500 g) peeled and deveined shrimp, finely chopped

1 egg white

2 tablespoons ground pork fat or fatty bacon, chopped

2 tablespoons fresh water chestnuts, peeled and finely chopped

1 tablespoon finely chopped scallions (white part only)

1 tablespoon light soy sauce

1 tablespoon Chinese rice wine

1 tablespoon peanut or vegetable oil

1 teaspoon tapioca starch

1 teaspoon salt

dash white pepper

DOUGH

1 1/2 cups sifted wheat starch

1/2 cup sifted tapioca flour

1 1/2 cups hot water

2 tablespoons peanut or vegetable oil

1. To make the Filling: Combine the shrimp, egg white, pork fat, water chestnuts, scallions, soy sauce, rice wine, oil, tapioca starch, salt, and pepper in a large bowl, stirring in one direction and mixing thoroughly. Cover and refrigerate at least 1 hour.

2. To make the Dough: Sift together the wheat starch and tapioca flour into a large mixing bowl. Gradually add the hot water, stirring constantly. Stir in the peanut oil. Let the dough cool a little, then knead until soft and smooth. Divide the dough in half. Keep one half covered in a bowl and place the other half on a lightly oiled surface. Knead, then roll into a sausagelike shape about 1 inch (2.5 cm) in diameter. Cut crosswise into about 36 pieces, 1/2 inch (1.5 cm) wide. Cover with a dry cloth to prevent the dough from drying out. Repeat with the remaining dough.

3. Brush some oil on one side of a cleaver, then flatten each small piece of dough with the blade by pressing evenly on the cleaver with the palm of your hand until the dough is very thin and about 2 1/2 inches (6 cm) in diameter. (A small oiled rolling pin may be used to roll out the dough instead of a cleaver.)

4. Place 1 heaping teaspoon shrimp filling in the center of one dough round. Fold the edges together, pleating on one side. Repeat with remaining filling and dough rounds.

5.   In batches, place the dumplings in a lightly greased steamer set or a bamboo steamer placed in a wok over water. Bring the water to a boil, cover, and steam 5 minutes, until the dumplings are cooked through. Serve directly from the steamer.

DOUGH TIP Hot water should be added very gradually to the dough, with constant stirring and mixing. If the water is too hot, the dough will be too elastic; if the water is too cool, the dough will crack.

STEAMED *SHAO MAI*

These open-faced shrimp/pork dumplings are delectable appetizers or hors d'oeuvres. They are one of the most popular dim sum served in tea houses in China. **Makes about 60 *shao mai*.**

1 package round wonton wrappers (60), thawed if frozen

FILLING
6 dried Chinese mushrooms

1¹/₂ cups Chinese cabbage, finely chopped

2 teaspoons salt

1 pound (500 g) ground pork

¹/₄ pound (125 g) peeled and deveined shrimp, cut into ¹/₄-inch (6-mm) dice

6 to 8 fresh water chestnuts, peeled and chopped

2 tablespoons chicken broth

2 tablespoons sesame oil

2 tablespoons soy sauce

1 tablespoon Chinese rice wine

1 tablespoon tapioca starch

1 tablespoon finely chopped gingerroot

1 scallion, finely chopped

¹/₂ teaspoon sugar

1. Remove the wonton wrappers from the package and cover with wet towels for 15 minutes before use.

2. To make the Filling: Soak the dried mushrooms in hot water until soft, 20 minutes; drain. Discard the stems; dice the caps. Place the chopped cabbage in a mixing bowl and sprinkle with 1 teaspoon salt. Mix well and let stand for 10 minutes. Squeeze the excess water from the cabbage with both hands.

3. In a large bowl, combine the diced mushrooms, pork, shrimp, water chestnuts, broth, sesame oil, soy sauce, rice wine, tapioca starch, gingerroot, scallion, sugar, and remaining 1 teaspoon salt; mix well. Add the chopped cabbage and mix thoroughly.

4. Place about 1 tablespoon filling in center of one wonton wrapper. With a wet finger, moisten the dough around the filling. Gather the sides of the wrapper around the filling, letting the wrapper form small pleats naturally. Squeeze the middle gently to make sure the wrapper sticks firmly against the filling and press down on a flat surface so that the *shao mai* flattens and can stand with the filling exposed at the top. (See illustrations at right.) Repeat with remaining wrappers and filling to make about 60 *shao mai*.

5. Place the *shao mai* in a lightly greased steamer set or bamboo steamer placed in a wok over water. Bring the water to a boil, cover, and steam 15 to 20 minutes, until cooked through. Serve directly from the steamer.

DO AHEAD The uncooked *shao mai* can be made in advance and frozen for several weeks. They can also be kept, covered, in the refrigerator for 2 to 3 days.

POT STICKERS

The Chinese name for these delectable dumplings, *guo tie*, literally means "pot stickers"—because the dumplings are not deep-fried, but only browned in oil on the bottom and then steam-cooked with chicken broth. The result is delicious dumplings crispy on the bottom and fluffy soft on the top. They can also be deep-fried, if you prefer. **Makes about 48 dumplings.**

DIPPING SAUCE (OPTIONAL)
1/4 cup soy sauce

2 tablespoons Chin Kiang vinegar

DOUGH
4 cups sifted all-purpose flour

1 cup boiling water

2/3 cup cold water

FILLING
3 to 5 dried Chinese mushrooms

1/2 pound (250 g) Chinese cabbage, finely chopped

3 1/2 teaspoons salt

1 pound (500 g) ground pork

1/4 pound (125 g) peeled and deveined shrimp, cut into 1/4-inch (6-mm) pieces

2 tablespoons dark soy sauce

2 tablespoons sesame oil

2 tablespoons chicken broth

1 tablespoon Chinese rice wine

1 teaspoon finely chopped gingerroot

3 tablespoons peanut or vegetable oil

1/2 cup chicken broth

1. To make the Dipping Sauce, if desired: Combine the soy sauce and vinegar in a small bowl; set aside.

2. To make the Dough: Place the flour in a large bowl; gradually pour in the boiling water while stirring with chopsticks. Gradually stir in the cold water. Knead until a smooth and soft dough results. Cover with a damp towel and let stand 15 minutes.

3. To make the Filling: Soak the mushrooms in hot water until soft, 20 minutes; drain. Discard the stems and chop the caps. Place the chopped cabbage in a bowl and sprinkle with 2 teaspoons salt. Mix well and let stand 10 minutes. Squeeze the excess water from the cabbage with both hands. In a large bowl, combine the chopped mushrooms, cabbage, pork, shrimp, soy sauce, sesame oil, broth, rice wine, gingerroot, and remaining 1 1/2 teaspoons salt. Mix thoroughly.

4. On a floured surface, knead the dough until smooth, 2 to 3 minutes. Divide into two parts. With your hands, firmly shape each piece into a sausagelike cylinder about 12 inches (30 cm) long and 1 inch (2.5 cm) in diameter. Cut the rolls of dough crosswise into 1/2-inch (1.5-cm) slices. Lay the slices on a lightly floured surface. Flatten each slice with the palm of your hand; roll with a rolling pin into rounds about 3 inches (7.5 cm) in diameter and about 1/8 inch (3 mm) thick.

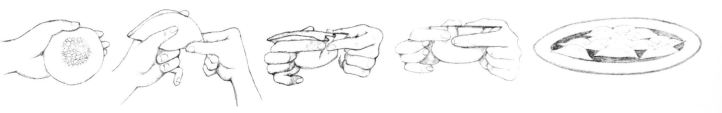

5.   Place about 2 teaspoons filling in the center of one round; fold over to make a half circle and pinch and pleat the edges together. (See illustrations above.) Transfer to a floured tray and cover with a dry towel. Repeat to make 48 dumplings.

6.   Heat a 12-inch (30-cm) skillet over high heat. Add 2 tablespoons oil and swirl in the pan. In batches, place the dumplings, pleated side up and sides just touching, in the pan. Fry over medium heat about 2 minutes, until the bottoms brown lightly. Add the broth, cover, and cook over medium heat about 10 minutes, until the liquid has been absorbed and the dumplings are cooked through.

7.   Add the remaining 1 tablespoon oil to the side of the pan and gently swirl it in the skillet. Let the dumplings cook, uncovered, 2 minutes longer. Place a round serving plate over the frying pan and invert the pan quickly. Serve the pot stickers (with the Dipping Sauce, if you like) as soon as they are finished.

DO AHEAD The uncooked dumplings can be made in advance and kept in the refrigerator for several hours. They can also be kept in the freezer for several weeks.

STEAMED DUMPLINGS

This is a famous Northern-style dumpling dish. Hot water and a little oil are used to make the soft, delicate dough. Unflavored gelatin makes the filling very juicy. **Makes about 30 dumplings.**

DOUGH

about 2 cups all-purpose flour

$^3/_4$ cup plus 2 tablespoons boiling water

1 tablespoon peanut or vegetable oil

FILLING

1 cup finely chopped Chinese cabbage

1 teaspoon salt

$^1/_2$ pound (250 g) ground pork

2 tablespoons chicken broth

1 tablespoon dark soy sauce

1 tablespoon Chinese rice wine

1 tablespoon sesame oil

1 scallion, finely chopped

1 teaspoon finely chopped gingerroot

1 envelope unflavored gelatin

1.   To make the Dough: Place 2 cups flour in a large bowl; gradually pour in the boiling water while stirring with chopsticks. Add the oil; stir until the flour is damp and mealy. Let the dough cool, then knead until soft and smooth, adding additional flour if it is too sticky. Cover the dough with a damp cloth and let stand 15 minutes.

2.   To make the Filling: Place the chopped cabbage in a bowl and sprinkle with $^1/_2$ teaspoon salt. Mix well and let stand for 10 minutes. Squeeze the excess water from the cabbage with both hands. In a large bowl, combine the ground pork, broth, soy sauce, rice wine, sesame oil, scallion, gingerroot, gelatin, and remaining $^1/_2$ teaspoon salt; mix well. Add the cabbage and thoroughly mix.

3.   Knead the dough again and divide into two parts. Keep one half covered and shape the other half into a sausagelike cylinder about 1 inch ($2^1/_2$ cm) in diameter. Cut into 15 pieces. Dust both sides of each piece with flour and press down with the palm of your hand. Roll with a rolling pin into a round about $2^1/_2$ inches (6 cm) in diameter and $^1/_8$ inch (3 mm) thick.

4.   Place about 1 tablespoon filling in the center of one round; fold the dough over to make a half circle and pinch and pleat the edges together. (See illustrations page 27.) Repeat with the remaining dough and filling to make 30 dumplings.

5.   Line a steamer set or bamboo steamer placed in a wok over water with slightly damp cheesecloth; arrange the dumplings on the cloth. Bring the water to a boil, cover, and steam 15 minutes, until the dumplings are cooked through. Serve directly from the steamer.

DO AHEAD The uncooked dumplings can be placed on the steamer and refrigerated for several hours until ready to steam.

PEKING DUMPLINGS WITH PORK AND VEGETABLES

In China, these dumplings—called *shui jiao*—are usually served as a main course, but they also make terrific dim sum. The dumplings are often served at the New Year to symbolize wealth. Makes about 50 to 60 dumplings.

1 package round wonton wrappers
(50 to 60), thawed if frozen

DIPPING SAUCE
2 tablespoons soy sauce

1 tablespoon Chin Kiang vinegar

chili oil, or mashed garlic cloves to
taste

FILLING
3/4 pound (375 g) Chinese cabbage,
finely chopped

1 teaspoon salt

1 pound (500 g) ground pork

3 tablespoons dark soy sauce

2 tablespoons sesame oil

2 tablespoons chicken broth

1 tablespoon Chinese rice wine

1 tablespoon finely chopped
gingerroot

2 scallions, chopped

1. Remove the wonton wrappers from the package and cover with wet towels for 15 minutes before use.

2. To make the Dipping Sauce: In a small bowl, combine the soy sauce, vinegar, and chili oil. Set aside.

3. To make the Filling: Place the chopped cabbage in a mixing bowl and sprinkle with the salt. Mix well and let stand for 10 minutes. Squeeze the excess water from the cabbage with both hands. In a large bowl, combine the pork, soy sauce, sesame oil, broth, rice wine, gingerroot, and scallions; mix thoroughly. Stir in the chopped cabbage.

4. Place about 1 tablespoon filling in center of one wonton wrapper. With a wet finger, moisten the edges and fold over to make a half circle and pleat edges together. Press with your finger to make sure it is tightly sealed. (See illustrations page 27.) Repeat to make remaining dumplings.

5. Bring 8 cups water to boil in a large pot. Drop the dumplings, one by one, into the boiling water; stir to make sure they do not stick to the bottom. Cook for about 30 seconds or until the water boils again. Add 2/3 cup cold water. When it boils again, add another 2/3 cup cold water. When the water boils again, the dumplings are ready. Transfer the dumplings with a wire sieve to a plate.

DO AHEAD The dumplings can be made ahead of time and frozen before cooking. No need to defrost before cooking.

VARIATION These dumplings can be deep-fried, rather than boiled. Heat 3 1/2 cups oil in wok over high heat. Reduce heat to medium. In batches, add dumplings and deep-fry until golden brown.

SHRIMP LAVER ROLLS

This is a beautiful dish and excellent for hors d'oeuvres and dim sum. To make ginger juice, use a garlic press to squeeze the juice from a piece of peeled ginger root. **Makes about 18 rolls.**

SHRIMP AND MARINADE
$1/2$ pound (500 g) peeled and
 deveined shrimp

3 ounces (90 g) pork fat, ground

$1/2$ egg white

1 tablespoon gingerroot juice

$1^1/2$ teaspoons Chinese rice wine

1 teaspoon tapioca starch

$1/2$ teaspoon salt

1 scallion, finely chopped

3 laver (dried seaweed, see below)
 sheets at least $7^1/2$ by $7^1/2$
 inches, soaked in cold water

2 cups peanut oil or vegetable oil

$1/2$ pound (250 g) bok choy, cut
 into 1-inch (2.5-cm) pieces

$1^1/2$ teaspoons Chinese rice wine

$1/2$ teaspoon salt

$1/4$ teaspoon sugar

1. To make the marinade: On a cutting board, crush the shrimp with one side of a cleaver. Add the ground pork fat and finely chop the mixture. Combine the egg white, gingerroot juice, rice wine, tapioca starch, salt, and scallion in a large bowl. Add the shrimp mixture and marinate 30 minutes.

2. Cut each sheet of seaweed into 6 pieces. Place about $1^1/2$ teaspoons shrimp mixture near a long edge of one sheet; roll into a tight roll about the size of an index finger. Squeeze gently so that the shrimp mixture extends a bit out both ends. Use a little shrimp mixture to seal the outer edge of the roll. Set aside. Repeat with remaining shrimp mixture and seaweed sheets to make 18 rolls.

3. Heat 2 tablespoons oil in a wok over medium-high heat. Add the bok choy and stir-fry briefly. Add the rice wine, salt, and sugar and stir-fry about 2 minutes, until the bok choy is tender. Spoon onto the middle of a large serving platter.

4. Heat the remaining oil in the wok over medium-high heat. Add the laver rolls and deep-fry over medium heat 2 minutes, until cooked through. With a slotted spoon, transfer the rolls to paper towels to drain, then arrange around the bok choy on the platter.

SUBSTITUTE Uncooked watercress can be used instead of bok choy as the green in the center of the plate.

ABOUT LAVER Laver is dried seaweed that has been pressed into sheets as thin as transparent rice paper. Rich in iodine and sea flavor, it is often used in quick soups. You can find purple laver sheets in Asian markets.

SHANGHAI SPRING ROLLS

These traditional spring rolls are long and thin and much more delicate than the "egg rolls" served in U.S. restaurants or available in supermarkets. They are excellent dim sum and a popular dish at traditional Chinese buffet dinners. Makes about 25 spring rolls.

DIPPING SAUCE (OPTIONAL)
2 tablespoons light soy sauce

1 tablespoon Chin Kiang vinegar

PORK AND MARINADE
1 tablespoon dark soy sauce

$1^1/_2$ teaspoons Chinese rice wine

1 teaspoon tapioca starch

$^1/_2$ pound (250 g) lean pork, sliced or shredded into small pieces

FILLING
8 to 10 dried Chinese mushrooms

2 tablespoons vegetable oil

$^1/_2$ pound (250 g) Chinese cabbage, shredded

$^1/_2$ cup chicken broth

$1^1/_2$ tablespoons dark soy sauce

$^1/_2$ teaspoon salt

$^1/_2$ pound (250 g) bean sprouts, rinsed and drained

$1^1/_2$ tablespoons tapioca starch dissolved in 2 tablespoons water

FLOUR PASTE
$^1/_4$ cup flour

6 tablespoons water

25 spring roll wrappers

$3^1/_2$ cups peanut or vegetable oil

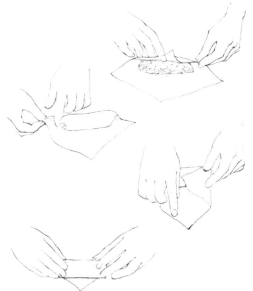

1. To make the Dipping Sauce, if you like: Combine the soy sauce and vinegar in a small bowl. Set aside.

2. To make the marinade: Combine the soy sauce, rice wine, and tapioca starch in a large bowl. Add the pork and marinate at least 30 minutes.

3. To make the Filling: Soak the mushrooms in hot water until soft, 20 minutes; drain. Discard the stems; shred the caps. Heat the oil in wok over medium-high heat; add the marinated pork and stir-fry 30 seconds. Transfer the pork with a slotted spoon to a plate. Add the cabbage to the wok and stir-fry for a moment. Add the shredded mushrooms, broth, soy sauce, and salt. Cover and cook 2 minutes. Return the pork to the wok, along with the bean sprouts, and stir-fry over high heat 30 seconds. Stir in the tapioca starch paste until the mixture is thickened. With a wire strainer, transfer the meat and vegetables to a plate to cool.

4. To make the spring rolls: Make the paste by combining the flour and water in a small bowl. When the filling is cool, place about 2 tablespoons filling diagonally along one corner of a spring

roll wrapper. Starting with the corner, roll tightly several times. Fold the right corner to center, then the left corner to center. Spread some paste on the final corner of the wrapper (to seal) and finish rolling into a tight roll. (See illustrations on page 34.) Repeat with the remaining wrappers and filling to make 25 rolls.

5.   Heat the peanut oil in wok over high heat. Reduce the heat to medium. In batches, add the spring rolls and deep-fry until golden brown. Serve hot with the dipping sauce, if you like.

FILLING TIPS It is important to wait until the filling is cool before you stuff and make the spring rolls. Make sure the filling is quite dry as well; otherwise the wrappers will soak through and tear.

DO AHEAD Cooled, fried spring rolls can be wrapped tightly and frozen. Before serving, reheat in a 350°F (177°C) oven for 15 to 20 minutes.

STEAMED ROAST PORK BUNS

In China, roast pork buns, known as *cha sio pao*, are served as breakfast, lunch, snacks, or dim sum. They are a favorite mid-afternoon snack for hungry children returning home from school. Doughy on the outside, the filling is mellow with the tasty diced roast pork. **Makes about 20 buns.**

DOUGH

about 3¹/₂ cups all-purpose flour

¹/₂ package active dry yeast (about 1 teaspoon)

¹/₄ cup lukewarm water

1 cup milk

2 tablespoons sugar

¹/₂ teaspoon baking powder

FILLING

¹/₂ cup water

1¹/₂ teaspoons all-purpose flour

1¹/₂ teaspoons tapioca starch

2 tablespoons dark soy sauce

1¹/₂ tablespoons sugar

1¹/₂ teaspoons oyster sauce

1¹/₂ teaspoons sesame oil

¹/₂ pound (250 g) Chinese roast pork (with some fat), thinly sliced and cut into ¹/₄-inch (6-mm) squares

1.   To make the Dough: Place the flour in a large mixing bowl. In a separate bowl, combine the yeast with the lukewarm water. In a small saucepan over medium heat, heat the milk until just warm. Remove from the heat, add the sugar, and stir to dissolve. Stir the yeast mixture into the milk. Slowly stir the milk mixture into the flour to form a soft, firm dough. Knead the dough until smooth; leave the dough in the bowl and cover with a damp cloth. Let rise in a warm place for 1¹/₂ to 2 hours, until doubled in bulk.

2.   To make the Filling: In a saucepan combine the water, flour, and tapioca starch. Stir to dissolve. Add the soy sauce, sugar, oyster sauce, and sesame oil. Heat and stir until the mixture thickens. Add the squares of roast pork and blend well. Let the filling cool.

3.   Punch down the dough and turn onto a lightly floured surface. Add the baking powder and knead for about 10 minutes, until the dough is smooth; sprinkle with flour from time to time while kneading. Roll the dough into a sausagelike roll 1¹/₂ inches (4 cm) in diameter. Cut into 20 pieces. With the palm of the hand, flatten each piece into a circle, then roll each with a small rolling pin to a 3-inch (7.5-cm) round, with the center of each round thicker than the edge.

4.   Place about 1 heaping tablespoon filling in the center of one round. Flute the edge of the round and gather together to form a pouch. (See illustrations at right.) Repeat to

make 20 buns. Set the buns on a square of waxed paper and cover with a damp towel as they are made. Let rise 30 minutes.

5.   Place the buns in a lightly greased steamer set or bamboo steamer placed in a wok over boiling water. Cover and steam 15 minutes, until cooked through.

DO AHEAD Steamed buns can be tightly wrapped and frozen for a month. Reheat by steaming for 15 to 20 minutes.

DEEP-FRIED SHRIMP BALLS

In China, these rich tidbits are often served as one of the main courses when entertaining. Because of their small size and delicate taste, they are also excellent dim sum. **Makes about 12 shrimp balls.**

PEPPERCORN SALT

1/4 cup salt or coarse salt

2 tablespoons Szechuan peppercorns

2 egg whites

3 ounces (90 g) ground pork fat or blanched fatty bacon

1 pound (500 g) peeled and deveined shrimp, chopped to a fine paste

1 tablespoon Chinese rice wine

1 tablespoon tapioca starch

1 teaspoon salt

1/8 teaspoon white pepper

1 (1/2-inch or 1-cm) piece fresh gingerroot

2 cups peanut or vegetable oil

1. To make the Peppercorn Salt: Heat the salt and Szechuan peppercorns in a dry pan over low heat. Stir until the salt is browned and the peppercorns are darkened and fragrant. Let cool, then crush with the wooden handle of the cleaver or grind in a blender. Strain through a fine sieve; set aside. (Peppercorn Salt keeps well in a tightly covered bottle.)

2. Beat the egg whites until foamy; add the ground pork fat and beat 2 minutes. Add the ground shrimp, rice wine, tapioca starch, salt, and pepper. With a garlic press, squeeze the juice from the gingerroot; add the juice to the shrimp mixture. Mix well.

3. Heat a wok over high heat until very hot. Add the oil and heat over medium heat. With your left hand, take a handful of the shrimp paste and squeeze your fingers into a fist. A ball about the size of a walnut will spurt from between your thumb and forefinger. With your right hand, use a measuring tablespoon dipped in cold water (to prevent sticking) to scoop up the shrimp ball and drop it into the hot oil. Repeat to make about 12 balls. Fry the shrimp balls, turning frequently to cook evenly, about 2 minutes, or until they float to the top and become fluffy. Do not overcook; overfrying will shrink the shrimp balls. Transfer the balls to a paper towel–lined plate to drain. Serve hot with Peppercorn Salt.

DO AHEAD The shrimp paste can be kept covered in the refrigerator for a few hours or overnight. The cooked shrimp balls can be frozen and reheated in a preheated 350°F (177°C) oven.

STEAMED PEARL BALLS

After being steamed, the glutinous rice coating on these crunchy meatballs becomes beautifully white and shiny, and the balls resemble large pearls. They make excellent dim sum—and are especially beautiful when served directly from a bamboo steamer. **Makes about 30 pearl balls.**

$^2/_3$ cup glutinous rice (sweet rice)

4 to 6 dried Chinese mushrooms

1 pound (500 g) ground pork

1 egg

1 tablespoon light soy sauce

$1^1/_4$ teaspoons salt

$^1/_4$ teaspoon sugar

1 tablespoon tapioca starch dissolved in 2 tablespoons water

6 to 8 fresh water chestnuts, peeled and finely chopped

1 scallion, finely chopped

1. Rinse and then soak the glutinous rice for at least 3 hours. Drain and spread out on a cloth towel to dry, about 30 minutes. Soak the mushrooms in hot water until soft, 20 minutes; drain. Discard the stems and finely chop the caps.

2. In a mixing bowl, combine the ground pork, egg, soy sauce, salt, and sugar. Stir in the tapioca starch and water mixture and mix well. Add the mushrooms, water chestnuts, and scallion and mix again.

3. Scoop up about $1^1/_2$ tablespoons of the pork mixture with a wet hand and shape it into a ball about 1 inch (2.5 cm) in diameter. Repeat to make about 30 balls. One at a time, roll the balls in the glutinous rice and place in a lightly oiled steamer basket. Cover and refrigerate until ready to steam.

4. Place the pearl balls in a lightly greased steamer set or bamboo steamer placed in a wok over water. Bring the water to a boil, cover, and steam 20 to 25 minutes, until cooked through. Serve hot.

VARIATIONS For those who prefer, ground veal or beef can be used but the flavor will not be as good.

DO AHEAD The pearl balls can be frozen for future use. Just defrost, then heat them up by steaming for about 15 minutes.

SCALLOPS AND CHINESE RADISH BALLS

For those who have never had Chinese radishes, this recipe offers a pleasant introduction. The round radish balls acquire a translucent look after being boiled and soaked in cold water. They are lovely to look at surrounded by the white glazed sauce and the yellow scallop shreds. **Makes about 30 Chinese Radish Balls.**

$1^1/_2$ ounces (45 g) dried scallops

$1^1/_2$ cups hot chicken broth

2 Chinese radishes, about 2 pounds (1 kg)

2 tablespoons peanut or vegetable oil

1 slice gingerroot

1 tablespoon Chinese rice wine

$^1/_2$ teaspoon salt

1 tablespoon tapioca starch dissolved in $1^1/_2$ tablespoons water

1.   Soak the dried scallops in $^1/_2$ cup of the hot broth for about 30 minutes. Steam scallops with broth for about 30 minutes. When cool, shred the scallops with fingers. Save the broth for later use.

2.   Use a small melon ball scoop to cut the radishes into about 30 small balls. In a pot of boiling water, cook the radish balls about 10 minutes; drain and soak in cold water.

3.   Heat the oil in wok over medium-high heat. Add the gingerroot slice and radish balls and stir-fry a few seconds. Add the shredded scallops with their broth, the rice wine, salt, and remaining 1 cup broth. Cook over low heat 1 minute. Stir in the tapioca starch mixture and cook briefly, until thickened. Serve hot.

SUBSTITUTION Dried scallops are very tasty and expensive (even though a little goes a long way). Dried shrimp can be used instead of dried scallops. Soak and steam dried shrimp as directed for the dried scallops but do not shred or cut the shrimp.

DO AHEAD The preparation for this dish can be done ahead of time through step 2. The final step takes but a few minutes.

FISH WRAPPED IN TOFU SKIN

In this favorite dim sum from the eastern shores of China, pieces of white fish are wrapped in tofu skin—also known as dried bean curd sheets. Tofu skin, large half-moon-shaped sheets, are very brittle and should be handled with care. **Makes about 12 dim sum servings.**

PEPPERCORN SALT
$1/4$ cup salt or coarse salt

2 tablespoons Szechuan peppercorns

FILLING
$1/2$ pound (250 g) sole, pike, or flounder fillet, cut into $1^1/2$-inch-long (4-cm) julienne strips

1 teaspoon Chinese rice wine

$1/2$ teaspoon salt

$1/4$ teaspoon sugar

dash white pepper

PASTE
$1/2$ lightly beaten egg

3 tablespoons cold water

2 tablespoons flour

$1/4$ teaspoon salt

2 teaspoons minced scallion

6 pieces tofu (dried bean curd) skin

2 cups peanut or vegetable oil

1. To make the Peppercorn Salt: Heat the salt and Szechuan peppercorns in a dry pan over low heat. Stir until the salt is browned and the peppercorns are darkened and fragrant. Let cool, then crush with the wooden handle of the cleaver or grind in a blender. Strain through a fine sieve; set aside. (Peppercorn Salt keeps well in a tightly covered bottle.)

2. To make the Filling: Combine the fish, rice wine, salt, sugar, and white pepper. Refrigerate 30 minutes. To make the thin Paste: Combine the egg, water, flour, salt, and scallion, in a small bowl. Set aside.

3. Handling the dried bean curd skin carefully, place each sheet between damp cloths. Set aside for 15 to 20 minutes, until they are soft enough to handle. (Sprinkle water on them if necessary to make them soft.)

4. Brush each softened skin lightly with the paste. Loosely stack the skins in two piles of three skins, so that each rounded edge extends 2 inches (5 cm) beyond the skin above it. Divide the filling into 2 portions. Take one portion of the filling and place it along the straight side of the top tofu skin. Loosely cover the filling with the straight side of the tofu skin, tuck in both ends, and roll until the skin is entirely rolled up into a 10-inch (25-cm) cylinder. (See illustrations below.) Repeat with the remaining stack of tofu skins and filling.

5.   Using a sharp cleaver, cut each roll diagonally into $1^1/_2$-inch-long (4-cm-long) sections. In a wok over medium-high heat, heat the oil until hot. In batches, add a few pieces of the rolls and fry 3 to 4 minutes, until golden and crispy. Drain well on paper towels. Serve hot with the Peppercorn Salt.

DO AHEAD The recipe can be completed through step 4 and the rolls can be refrigerated, covered, for 4 to 5 hours.

VARIATION For a tasty vegetarian dim sum, wrap shredded, rehydrated dried mushrooms, bamboo shoots, and bean sprouts, stir-fried with light soy sauce and sugar, in the tofu skins and deep-fry.

SHRIMP TOAST

Crunchy and tasty, shrimp toast is an excellent finger food to be served as dim sum or hors d'oeuvres. In China, it is usually served as a snack or as one of the main dishes in a buffet dinner. Makes about 24 shrimp toasts.

$1/2$ pound (250 g) peeled and deveined shrimp, chopped to a fine paste

6 fresh water chestnuts, peeled and finely chopped

2 tablespoons ground pork fat or fatty bacon

1 egg, lightly beaten

1 tablespoon Chinese rice wine

1 tablespoon tapioca starch

1 teaspoon salt

$1/2$ teaspoon sugar

1 ($1/2$-inch or 1.5-cm) piece gingerroot

6 slices white bread (at least 2 days old), crusts trimmed

24 leaves fresh Chinese parsley

2 cups peanut or vegetable oil

1. In a medium bowl, combine the minced shrimp, water chestnuts, pork fat, egg, rice wine, tapioca starch, salt, and sugar. With a garlic press, squeeze the juice from the gingerroot; add the juice to the mixture. Mix thoroughly to form a paste.

2. Cut each slice of bread into 4 triangles. Spread about 1 teaspoon shrimp mixture on each triangle and top with 1 parsley leaf.

3. Heat the oil in a wok to 375°F (182°C) over medium-high heat. In batches, gently lower the bread triangles, shrimp side down, into the oil; fry 1 minute. Turn the toasts over and fry few seconds longer, until golden brown. Drain on paper towels and serve immediately.

DO AHEAD The fried shrimp toast can be frozen and then reheated in a preheated oven (375°F or 182°C) for 15 minutes.

ABOUT CHINESE PARSLEY This popular ingredient in Chinese cooking is more commonly known as cilantro or coriander leaves in the United States.

QUAIL EGGS IN BROWN SAUCE

This fancy vegetarian dish is often banquet fare for vegetarians and monks. Tiny golden brown quail eggs are mixed with straw mushrooms and yellow baby corn, then surrounded by crispy green snow peas—a delight to look at. **Makes about 8 dim sum servings.**

1 (15-ounce or 500-g) can quail eggs (see below)

2 tablespoons dark soy sauce

SEASONING SAUCE
$1/2$ cup chicken broth

1 tablespoon tapioca starch

1 teaspoon sugar

1 teaspoon salt

1 teaspoon sesame oil

$1^1/2$ cups peanut or vegetable oil for deep-frying

2 tablespoons flour

3 tablespoons peanut or vegetable oil for stir-frying

$1/2$ pound (250 g) fresh snow peas, blanched

1 (15-ounce or 500-g) can straw mushrooms, drained and rinsed

1 (15-ounce or 500-g) can baby corn, drained and rinsed

1. In a medium bowl, marinate the quail eggs in the soy sauce 10 minutes, turning the eggs frequently. Remove the quail eggs and set aside; reserve the soy sauce.

2. To make the Seasoning Sauce: To the soy sauce used to marinate the eggs, add the broth, tapioca starch, sugar, salt, and sesame oil; mix well. Set aside.

3. Heat the $1^1/2$ cups oil in a wok over medium heat. Meanwhile, coat the quail eggs with the flour. When the oil is hot, carefully add the eggs to the wok and deep-fry until golden brown. Set aside.

4. Discard the oil in the wok and wipe dry. Heat 1 tablespoon oil in the wok; add the snow peas and stir-fry for a few seconds. Add one-half of the seasoning sauce and stir-fry about 1 minute. Arrange the snow peas attractively around the outer edge of each dim sum serving plate.

5. Heat the remaining 2 tablespoons oil in the wok; add the straw mushrooms and baby corn and stir-fry for about 1 minute. Add the remaining seasoning sauce and mix thoroughly. Add the quail eggs and stir well. Transfer the eggs and vegetables to the center of the serving plates and serve.

ABOUT QUAIL EGGS Quail eggs (usually cooked, shelled, and canned), although unfamiliar to most Americans, have a delicate taste. Find them in Asian markets.

PAPER-WRAPPED CHICKEN

Chicken that is wrapped in paper and deep-fried retains its juice and flavor. It is also great fun to eat! After being deep-fried, the beautiful design—black mushroom, green parsley leaf, and red ham on white chicken slice—shows through the paper. Just be sure to remind your guests that the paper should be removed and discarded before eating. **Makes about 20 packages.**

CHICKEN AND MARINADE

1 tablespoon light soy sauce

1 tablespoon Chinese rice wine

$^1/_2$ teaspoon salt

$^1/_2$ teaspoon sugar

$^1/_4$ teaspoon white or black pepper

1 large whole chicken cutlet or 1 skinned and boned chicken breast (about $^3/_4$ to 1 pound or 375 to 500 g), cut into 1x2-inch (2.5x 5-cm) slices, $^1/_4$ inch (6 mm) thick

5 dried Chinese mushrooms

$^1/_2$ pound (250 g) Smithfield ham, fat trimmed

2 tablespoons sesame oil

20 Chinese parsley leaves

2 cups peanut or vegetable oil

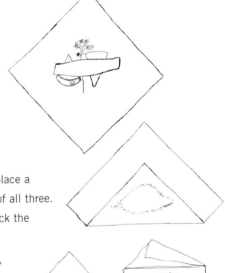

1.   To make the marinade: Combine the soy sauce, rice wine, salt, sugar, and pepper. Add the chicken and marinate at least 20 minutes.

2.   Soak the mushrooms in hot water until soft, 20 minutes; drain. Discard the stems. Cut each mushroom into quarters.

3.   Boil the ham in a small pot of water 10 minutes. When cool, cut into small triangular shapes the same size as the mushrooms.

4.   Cut 20 (6x6-inch or 15x15-cm) pieces of cellophane paper. Brush sesame oil on 1 sheet of paper. Place 1 parsley leaf in the middle. Next to it, place a mushroom; on the other side, place a ham slice. Lay a strip of chicken on top of all three. Fold like an envelope into a rectangular package. (See illustrations at right.) Tuck the corner inside to make a neat package. Repeat to make 20 packages.

5.   Heat the oil in a wok over medium-low heat. In batches, add the packages, face down, and fry 2 minutes, until almost cooked through; turn the packages over and fry 30 seconds more. Drain and serve hot.

DO AHEAD The paper-wrapped chicken can be cooked ahead of time. To serve, warm in a preheated oven (350°F or 177°C) for about 15 minutes.

Princess Chicken

In this fancy chicken dish, the center section of the chicken wing, considered a delicacy by the Chinese, is stuffed with shredded mushrooms, ham, and bamboo shoots. These delicious and delicate wings can be served as dim sum, hors d'oeuvres, or a main dish. If served as dim sum, the vegetables (mushrooms, bamboo shoot slices, and snow peas) can be omitted. **Makes about 12 chicken wings.**

SEASONING SAUCE
2 tablespoons cold water

1 tablespoon oyster sauce

2 teaspoons light soy sauce

1 teaspoon tapioca starch

$1/2$ teaspoon sugar

CHICKEN WINGS AND
STUFFING
12 strips dried Chinese mushrooms,
  $2 \times 1/4 \times 1/4$-inch ($5 \times 1/2 \times 1/2$-cm)

12 large chicken wings

12 strips cooked Smithfield ham,
  $2 \times 1/4 \times 1/4$-inch ($5 \times 1/2 \times 1/2$-cm)

12 strips cup bamboo shoots,
  $2 \times 1/4 \times 1/4$-inch ($5 \times 1/2 \times 1/2$-cm)

MARINADE
1 tablespoon light soy sauce

1 tablespoon Chinese rice wine

$1/2$ teaspoon salt

4 to 6 dried Chinese mushrooms

2 tablespoons peanut or vegetable
  oil

2 slices gingerroot

2 scallions, cut into 2-inch (5-cm)
  lengths

$1/2$ cup bamboo shoots, thinly sliced

$1/4$ pound (125 g) snow peas or $1/4$
  cup green pepper, cut into 1-inch
  (2.5-cm) squares

1.   To make the Seasoning Sauce: Combine the water, oyster sauce, soy sauce, tapioca starch, and sugar; set aside.

2.   To prepare the stuffing ingredients: Soak the dried mushrooms until soft, 20 minutes; drain. From the chicken wings, cut off the wing tips and third sections; discard or reserve for other use. Chop off a small piece of bone at each end with a cleaver. Cook the boned wings in 2 cups boiling water 3 to 4 minutes. Drain the wings (reserving $1/2$ cup of the cooking water) and let sit until cool enough to handle.

3.   To stuff the chicken wings: When cool, sever the wing tendons at both ends of each wing and gently push the bones out with your fingers. Immediately place 1 strip each of mushroom, ham, and bamboo shoot into the cavity.

4.   To make the marinade: Combine the soy sauce, rice wine, and salt in a large bowl. Add the wings and marinate 20 to 30 minutes.

5.   To brown the chicken wings with vegetables: Soak the mushrooms in hot water until soft, 20 minutes; drain. Discard the stems. Cut the mushrooms into quarters. Heat the oil in a wok over high heat. Add the gingerroot and scallions and stir-fry for a few seconds. Add the wings and cook until browned, 2 to 3 minutes;

gently turn over and cook for 1 minute longer. Stir in the quartered mushrooms, bamboo shoot slices, and snow peas. Add the reserved $^1/_2$ cup cooking water and cook 2 minutes. Stir the seasoning sauce and add to the chicken and vegetables; stir until the sauce thickens and coats the wings with a clear glaze. Serve hot.

DO AHEAD The chicken wings can be stuffed in advance and refrigerated. The mushrooms, bamboo shoots, and snow peas can be sliced before cooking. These tasks done in advance will make the final preparation very short.

LION'S HEAD

In China, naming something after the king of the jungle implies both high quality and a large size. In this traditional dish, the "Lion's Head" is a large meatball, sitting on a bed of bok choy which symbolizes the lion's mane. Traditionally, Lion's Head is served on New Year's Day, although it is often served at other times of the year. Broken into pieces, the large meatballs make excellent dim sum servings. **Makes about 4 to 6 large meatballs.**

1 pound (500 g) ground pork

3 tablespoons dark soy sauce

$1/4$ cup tapioca starch dissolved in $1/2$ cup chicken broth

4 fresh water chestnuts, peeled and chopped

1 egg, lightly beaten

1 tablespoon Chinese rice wine

1 scallion, finely chopped

1 teaspoon finely chopped gingerroot

1 pound (500 g) bok choy

2 tablespoons peanut or vegetable oil

$1/2$ cup chicken broth

$1/2$ teaspoon sugar

1 tablespoon tapioca starch dissolved in 2 tablespoons cold water

1. In a large bowl, combine the ground pork, 2 tablespoons soy sauce, 1 tablespoon tapioca starch/broth mixture, the water chestnuts, egg, rice wine, scallion, and gingerroot. Shape the mixture into 4 to 6 balls. Set aside.

2. Cut each stalk of bok choy in half lengthwise; slice the pieces crosswise at 3-inch (7.5-cm) intervals. Arrange the bok choy in a layer on the bottom of a heavy 2- to 3-quart ovenproof casserole or large pot.

3. Heat the oil in a wok over medium-high heat. Give the remaining tapioca starch/chicken broth mixture a quick stir to recombine it. One by one, dip the meatballs into the tapioca starch to coat thoroughly and add to the wok. Cook the meatballs, turning once, until browned.

4. Gently transfer the meatballs to the bed of bok choy in the casserole. Add the remaining 1 tablespoon of soy sauce, the broth, and sugar and bring to a boil. Cover the casserole tightly, reduce the heat to low, and simmer for about 1 hour. Add additional water or broth if the casserole becomes too dry.

5. Arrange the bok choy on a platter with the meatballs on top. Add the 1 tablespoon tapioca starch mixed with 2 tablespoons water to the sauce remaining in the casserole; cook, stirring, until thickened. To serve as dim sum, break up the meatballs with a fork and serve pieces on individual plates, with a little sauce drizzled over each serving.

DO AHEAD Lion's Head can be made several hours before serving and simply reheated on top of the stove.

VARIATION For those who prefer not to eat pork, ground beef or veal can be used instead.

SPICED PORK

This is not a "spicy" dish at all—as the name would seem to indicate. In fact, it is rather sweet. The Chinese name translates as "bean sauce meat," because the pork is marinated in sweet bean sauce. Made from fermented soy beans, sweet bean sauce is similar to the more familiar hoisin sauce. Rock salt and sweet bean sauce can be found in Asian markets. **Makes about 8 dim sum servings.**

$1^1/_2$ pounds (750 g) fresh ham or boneless pork

3 tablespoons sweet bean sauce

3 tablespoons dark soy sauce

1 tablespoon Chinese rice wine

1 whole star anise

1 cup boiling water

$^1/_4$ cup rock sugar

1.   Wash the pork; wipe dry. Rub all sides with the sweet bean sauce; marinate 2 to 3 hours in the refrigerator.

2.   Place the soy sauce, wine, and star anise in a deep pot and bring to a boil; add the pork and boiling water. Simmer over low heat 30 minutes. Add the rock sugar and continue to simmer 1 hour longer, turning the meat frequently.

3.   When the sauce has been reduced to $^1/_2$ cup and is rather thick, remove the pot from the heat and let the meat cool in the pot.

4.   Slice the pork and arrange it attractively on a plate. Pour the thick dark sauce on top.

DO AHEAD This dish is excellent for buffet dinners or large parties since it can be done totally ahead of time and served at room temperature.

SWEET AND SOUR SPARERIBS

Like many dim sum dishes, these succulent ribs, cooked by the Chinese "red-cooking" method, can be served either as small bites or as a main dish. **Makes about 8 dim sum servings.**

1 tablespoon peanut or vegetable oil

2 slices gingerroot

2 scallions, cut into 2-inch (5-cm) pieces

$1^1/_2$ pounds (750 g) spareribs (ask your butcher to cut across the bones into $1^1/_2$-inch or 4-cm sections), ribs separated

$1/_4$ cup dark soy sauce

$1/_4$ cup sugar

$2^1/_2$ tablespoons Chin Kiang vinegar

$1^1/_2$ tablespoons Chinese rice wine

3 to 4 Chinese cabbage leaves, shredded

1.   Heat the oil in a Dutch oven or medium-size pot over medium-high heat. Add the gingerroot and scallions and stir. Add the spareribs and stir-fry 1 minute to brown them slightly.

2.   Add the soy sauce, sugar, vinegar, and wine. Bring to a boil and reduce the heat to low; cover and simmer, stirring occasionally, about 45 minutes.

3.   Arrange the shredded Chinese cabbage leaves on each dim sum plate and top with the spareribs; serve hot.

DO AHEAD The dish can be prepared ahead of time through step 2 and left in the pot. Reheat thoroughly on the stove before serving.

ABOUT CHIN KIANG VINEGAR Made from fermented rice, Chin Kiang vinegar has a rich, smokey taste. It is one of the black vinegars, and gets its name from the Chinese province where it is made. Find it in Asian food stores.

SPARERIBS WITH FERMENTED BLACK BEANS

Spareribs are first seared in hot oil to seal in the juices, then steam-cooked vigorously with fermented (salted) black beans, rice wine, and soy sauce. The result is tender, succulent ribs, full of rich flavor. Delicious as dim sum, they are also excellent when served as hors d'oeuvres or a main dish. Makes about 10 dim sum servings.

RIBS AND MARINADE

1/4 cup dark soy sauce

1 tablespoon sugar

2 pounds (1 kg) spareribs (ask your butcher to cut across bones into 1 1/2-inch or 4-cm sections), ribs separated

2 tablespoons peanut or vegetable oil

2 cloves garlic, crushed

1 cup water

2 tablespoons Chinese rice wine

1 1/2 tablespoons fermented black beans, coarsely chopped

1 teaspoon tapioca starch dissolved in 1 tablespoon water

1.   To make the marinade: Combine the soy sauce and sugar in a large bowl. Add the spareribs and marinate 20 minutes. Drain the ribs, reserving the marinade.

2.   Heat a wok over medium-high heat until very hot. Add the oil and heat through. Add the garlic and spareribs and stir-fry until the spareribs are lightly browned on both sides, about 1 minute. Add the reserved marinade, the water, rice wine, and black beans. Bring to a boil and reduce the heat to low. Cover and simmer, stirring 2 or 3 times, for about 1 hour.

3.   Stir the tapioca starch and water mixture and add to the wok; cook, stirring, until the sauce thickens. Serve hot.

DO AHEAD The ribs can be cooked ahead of time through step 2 and left in the wok. Just before serving, bring to a boil to heat the spareribs through, then stir in the tapioca starch/water mixture to thicken the sauce.

SPARERIBS STEAMED WITH SPICY RICE POWDER

When marinated spareribs are coated with spicy rice powder and then slowly steamed, the ribs become tender and moist, with a subtle spicy flavor. **Makes about 8 dim sum servings.**

RIBS AND MARINADE
1 scallion, shredded

2 tablespoons dark soy sauce

1 tablespoon Chinese rice wine

1 teaspoon sugar

$1/2$ teaspoon salt

$1/8$ teaspoon ground roasted Szechuan peppercorns (see below)

$1/8$ teaspoon dried red pepper, chopped

$1^1/2$ pounds (750 g) spareribs (ask your butcher to cut across bones into $1^1/2$-inch or 4-cm sections), ribs separated

$2/3$ cup spicy rice powder (see below)

bok choy leaves

1 scallion, shredded

1. To make the marinade: Mix the scallion, soy sauce, rice wine, sugar, salt, peppercorns, and dried red pepper in a large bowl; stir well to dissolve the salt and sugar. Add the spareribs and marinate 20 to 30 minutes, turning and mixing several times. Drain the ribs, reserving the marinade.

2. Coat each sparerib with spicy rice powder. Line a steamer set or a bamboo steamer with bok choy leaves. Place the bamboo steamer in a large wok over water. Arrange the ribs and shredded scallion in the steamer, making 2 layers at the most. Pour the reserved marinade on top. Bring the water to a boil, cover and steam the ribs $1^1/2$ hours, adding additional water as it boils off. Check after 1 hour of steaming; if some spicy rice powder coating the ribs is still dry, turn ribs around and continue steaming until all the rice powder coating is moist. Serve hot.

STEAMING TIP When steaming for long periods of time, always check to see that there is enough water under the steamer. Have a kettle of boiling water ready on the stove to add to the steamer when it needs more water.

GROUND ROASTED PEPPERCORNS To make the ground-roasted Szechuan peppercorns: Stir about $1/4$ cup of Szechuan peppercorns in a wok or saucepan, without oil, over medium heat for about 2 minutes or until they are lightly browned. Crush the peppercorns to a fine powder and store in a glass jar.

ABOUT SPICY RICE POWDER Spicy rice powder is an important element to this dish. If you can't find it in your local Asian market, you can make it yourself: Place some uncooked rice and star anise in a dry pan. Toast over medium heat until the rice is browned, but not scorched. Grind the mixture in a blender or coffee bean grinder to the consistency of coarse sand.

STUFFED CHINESE MUSHROOMS

This dish is truly a delicacy and can be served either as dim sum or a main dish. The chopped fresh water chestnuts add a crunchiness that contrasts nicely with the soft but tasty mushrooms. Makes about 40 stuffed mushrooms.

40 dried Chinese mushrooms, 1 to 1¹/₂ inches (2.5 to 4 cm) in diameter

FILLING
¹/₂ pound (250 g) ground pork

6 to 10 fresh water chestnuts, peeled and finely chopped

1 tablespoon dark soy sauce

1 tablespoon Chinese rice wine

1 teaspoon tapioca starch

¹/₂ teaspoon sugar

tapioca starch (to sprinkle on mushrooms)

40 small leaves fresh Chinese parsley

2 tablespoons peanut or vegetable oil

5 tablespoons oyster sauce

1. Soak the mushrooms in hot water to cover until soft, 20 minutes; drain, reserving the liquid. Strain the liquid and reserve ³/₄ cup. Discard the mushroom stems.

2. To make the Filling: In a medium bowl, combine the pork, water chestnuts, soy sauce, rice wine, tapioca starch, and sugar; mix thoroughly.

3. Sprinkle a little tapioca starch on the stem sides of the mushrooms; fill each with filling, smoothing it flat with a knife or your finger. Place a parsley leaf on top of each filled mushroom.

4. Heat the oil in a wok over high heat. Carefully arrange the mushrooms, stuffing side up, in a single layer in the wok. Reduce the heat to medium and cook until the mushrooms are lightly browned. Add the reserved mushroom water and oyster sauce, bring to a boil, and cover the wok. Reduce the heat to low and simmer 20 minutes, basting frequently, until the filling is cooked through. Transfer the mushrooms to a serving platter and pour the sauce over the mushrooms. Serve hot.

DO AHEAD The mushrooms can be prepared through step 3 and frozen for future use. They can also be cooked ahead of time, then refrigerated for later use. Reheat by pouring ¹/₄ cup mushroom water and 1 tablespoon oyster sauce into the wok and simmering for about 5 minutes.

STUFFED TOFU, CANTONESE STYLE

Here's a fancy way to eat nutritious tofu. It is a delicate and dainty dish, beautifully garnished with the glazed brown sauce and shredded green scallions. **Makes about 16 stuffed tofu triangles.**

4 cakes firm tofu

1 tablespoon dried shrimp

PORK AND MARINADE
1 tablespoon light soy sauce

1 tablespoon Chinese rice wine

1^1/$_2$ teaspoons tapioca starch

^{1}/$_4$ teaspoon salt

^{1}/$_4$ pound (125 g) ground pork

1 scallion, chopped

^{1}/$_3$ cup peanut or vegetable oil

1 cup chicken broth

1 tablespoon dark soy sauce

1 tablespoon oyster sauce

1 tablespoon tapioca starch dissolved in 1 tablespoon cold water

2 scallions, shredded

1.   Press the tofu with a heavy weight or 2 or 3 chopping boards for about 30 minutes to reduce excess water. Soak the dried shrimp in hot water 20 to 30 minutes. Drain and finely chop.

2.   To make the marinade: Combine the soy sauce, wine, tapioca starch, and salt in a large bowl. Add the ground pork and mix to combine; marinate for at least 15 minutes. Mix in the chopped dried shrimp and chopped scallion.

3.   Cut each piece of tofu diagonally into 4 triangular pieces. Cut a slit on the long side of one tofu triangle. Take out some tofu and stuff the opening carefully with meat mixture. (See illustrations below.) Repeat to make 16 stuffed triangles.

4.   Heat the oil in a wok over medium-high heat. Arrange the tofu, slit side down, in the wok and fry 2 minutes, until browned. Add the broth, cover, and simmer 3 to 4 minutes. Carefully transfer the tofu triangles to a plate and arrange attractively.

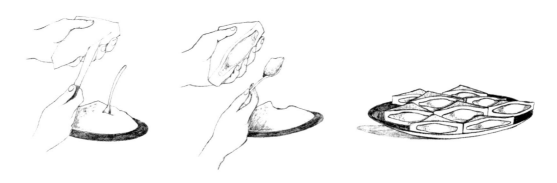

5.   Add the soy sauce and oyster sauce to the liquid in the wok and bring to a boil. Add the tapioca starch mixture and cook, stirring, until thickened. Pour the sauce over the tofu; garnish with the shredded scallions.

DO AHEAD The stuffed tofu can be browned and simmered ahead of time. Just before serving, reheat the tofu and its liquid in a wok or saucepan. Place the tofu pieces on a plate and thicken the sauce with the tapioca starch mixture.

ABOUT DRIED SHRIMP Dried shrimp are highly valued by the Chinese as a seasoning; you can find them in Asian markets. If you don't like their fishy smell, soak the dried shrimp overnight in rice wine.

STUFFED EGGPLANT

These deep-fried eggplant "sandwiches" are so delicious, it's hard to stop eating them. The coating is crispy, the eggplant tender, and the filling delectable. They are not only an excellent dim sum; they are equally popular as hors d'oeuvres or a fancy side dish. **Makes about 8 sandwiches.**

FILLING
1/4 cup dried shrimp
1/2 pound (250 g) ground pork
1 scallion, finely chopped
1 tablespoon dark soy sauce
1 tablespoon tapioca starch
1 tablespoon Chinese rice wine

1/2 teaspoon sugar
1/2 teaspoon salt
1/4 teaspoon pepper

1 medium-size eggplant or 3 to 4 small ones (about 1 pound or 500 g), peeled and cut into 16 1/8-inch (3-mm) slices

1 egg, beaten
1 cup bread crumbs
2 cups peanut or vegetable oil

1.   To make the Filling: Soak the dried shrimp in hot water 30 minutes. Drain and finely chop. Combine the dried shrimp, ground pork, scallion, soy sauce, tapioca starch, rice wine, sugar, salt, and pepper in a mixing bowl. Mix well.

2.   Spread about 1 tablespoon filling on one slice of eggplant and cover with another slice. Repeat to make 8 sandwiches. Dip each sandwich in the beaten egg, then dredge in the bread crumbs.

3.   Heat the oil in a wok over medium-high heat. In batches, add the eggplant sandwiches and fry 2 minutes on each side, until nicely browned. Slice each sandwich in half. Serve hot.

DO AHEAD The fried eggplant can be reheated in a 350°F (177°C) oven for 10 to 15 minutes.

STIR-FRIED RICE CAKES (NEW YEAR'S CAKES)

This dish is a must for a Chinese New Year's dinner or lunch, although it is served at other times as well. The Chinese name, *nien gao*, has special connotations: *Nien* means "year" and *gao* means "cake"—but *gao* also has same sound as the word for "high" or "tall," so *nien gao* symbolizes moving up higher and higher in position or career in the coming year. It is an excellent one-dish meal, but is also frequently served as dim sum. Makes about 8 dim sum servings.

1 pound (500 g) sliced dried rice cakes

6 dried Chinese mushrooms

SHRIMP AND MARINADE

1 teaspoon Chinese rice wine

1 teaspoon tapioca starch

$1/4$ teaspoon salt

$1/4$ pound (125 g) peeled and deveined shrimp, rinsed and patted dry

PORK AND MARINADE

1 tablespoon dark soy sauce

1 tablespoon Chinese rice wine

1 teaspoon tapioca starch

$1/2$ teaspoon sugar

1 cup shredded lean pork

6 tablespoons peanut or vegetable oil

$1/2$ cup bamboo shoots, shredded

3 cups shredded Chinese cabbage

1 teaspoon salt

$1/4$ cup red-in-snow preserved vegetables (see page 71), chopped

$1/3$ cup chicken broth

2 tablespoons dark soy sauce

1. Soak the dried rice cake slices in cold water overnight or at least 12 hours. Drain. Soak the mushrooms in hot water until soft, 20 minutes; drain. Discard the stems and shred the caps.

2. To make the shrimp marinade: Combine the rice wine, tapioca starch and salt in a medium bowl. Add the shrimp and marinate at least 30 minutes. To make the pork marinade: Combine the soy sauce, rice wine, tapioca starch, and sugar in another medium bowl. Add the shredded pork and marinate at least 30 minutes.

3. Heat a wok over high heat until very hot. Add 2 tablespoons oil and heat through. Add the shrimp and stir-fry until just cooked through, 1 minute. Transfer to a bowl and set aside. Heat another 2 tablespoons oil in the wok. Add the shredded pork and stir-fry until the color changes, about 1 minute. Add the shredded mushrooms and mix well; transfer to another bowl and set aside.

4. Heat 2 tablespoons oil in same wok. Add the bamboo shoots and Chinese cabbage and stir-fry 1 minute. Add the salt and mix well. Return the pork mixture to the wok, along with the chopped red-in-snow vegetables; cook 1 minute. Add the drained rice cake slices and sprinkle the broth and soy sauce on the rice cakes. Stir-fry until the cake slices are limp. Stir in the cooked shrimp, heat through, and serve hot.

VARIATION Four or five pieces of fresh rice cake may be used instead of the dried cakes and shredded beef or chicken may be used instead of pork. Fresh rice cakes must be soaked and sliced before use.

DO AHEAD This dish can be covered with aluminum foil and kept warm in the oven for about half an hour.

ABOUT RED-IN-SNOW Red-in-snow is kind of pickled mustard green; it is often used as a seasoning in stir-fried dishes because it is remarkably refreshing and crisp and adds flavor to other ingredients. The name comes from the red roots of the greens, which become visible in the snow in early spring. Find red-in-snow in Asian markets.

Chinese Cabbage in Cream Sauce

This beautiful vegetable dish, covered with milky white sauce dotted with reddish chopped ham, is often served as a banquet dish, but small portions make nice little mouthfuls for dim sum. Smithfield ham is close in taste, texture, and color to the famous Chinese Kim Hua ham, which is traditionally used in this dish. **Makes about 8 dim sum servings.**

$1/4$ cup milk

$1^1/_2$ tablespoons tapioca starch

1 small piece cooked Smithfield ham

3 tablespoons peanut or vegetable oil

$1^1/_4$ pounds (625 g) Chinese cabbage, leaves separated and cut into $1 \times 2^1/_2$-inch (2.5×6-cm) strips

1 teaspoon salt

$1/2$ teaspoon sugar

$3/4$ cup chicken broth

1.   Combine the milk and tapioca starch in a small bowl; mix until thoroughly dissolved. Set aside.

2.   Trim the skin and fat from the ham. Boil in water 10 to 15 minutes. When cool, finely chop; reserve 2 tablespoons. (The rest can be saved for another use.)

3.   Heat the oil in the wok over high heat; reduce the heat to medium high. Add the cabbage and stir-fry about 1 minute, until the cabbage strips are thoroughly coated with oil. Add the salt and sugar, then pour in the broth and stir well. Bring to a boil, cover, and simmer over low heat 10 minutes.

4.   With a strainer, transfer the cabbage to a serving platter and arrange the strips in one direction or arrange the strips on each individual dim sum plate. Bring the cooking liquid in the wok to a boil. Give the tapioca starch and milk a quick stir to recombine and add to the wok. Cook, stirring, until the sauce thickens. Pour the sauce over the cabbage, sprinkle with the chopped ham, and serve.

DO AHEAD This dish can be cooked ahead of time through step 3, simmering the cabbage for 10 minutes. Just before serving, bring the cabbage and liquid to a boil again and continue with step 4 to finish the dish.

ABOUT SMITHFIELD HAM Smithfield ham can be made into a delightful dim sum or an appetizer for a formal dinner: Cut the skin and fat from Smithfield ham. Place in a saucepan and cover with water. Simmer the ham over low heat 30 minutes. Dissolve $1/4$ cup sugar in 2 cups of boiling water; when cool, add 2 tablespoons Chinese rice wine. Cut the ham with the grain into 2-inch-wide (5-cm) pieces and place in a large jar. Pour the sugar solution over the ham. Cover the jar and refrigerate. The sugar-soaked ham keeps indefinitely. To serve as an appetizer or dim sum, slice the ham, coat with honey, and steam for 20 minutes.

SWEET-FILLED WONTONS (GOLDEN SURPRISE)

End your dim sum meal with a sweet treat—these dessert wontons are sure to please. **Makes about 60 wontons.**

1 package wonton wrappers (60),
   thawed if frozen

1 package (8-ounce or 250-g)
   pitted red dates

$1/2$ cup water

2 tablespoons sesame seeds

$1/2$ cup dark corn syrup

2 cups peanut or vegetable oil

confectioners' sugar

1.   Remove the wonton wrappers from the package and cover with wet towels for 15 minutes before use.

2.   In a small saucepan over medium heat, combine the dates and water; bring to a simmer. Reduce the heat and cook about 20 minutes. Drain. With a spice or coffee bean grinder, grind the dates and sesame seeds. Moisten with the syrup.

3.   Place about $1/2$ teaspoon date and sesame seed mixture in the center of one wonton wrapper. Moisten the edge of the wrapper with some water and fold over at the center. Gently press the edges together. Fold in half again lengthwise and then pull the corners one over the other and press them together with a little water. (See illustrations, page 21.) A properly wrapped wonton resembles a nurse's cap. Repeat to make 60 wontons.

4.   Heat the oil in a wok over medium-high heat. In batches, add the wontons and deep-fry until golden brown. Transfer to paper towels and drain and cool slightly. Sprinkle with confectioners' sugar. Serve at room temperature.

DO AHEAD These sweet-filled wontons can be kept for several weeks in a tightly covered container.

BANANAS STUFFED WITH SWEET RED BEAN PASTE

Sweet red bean paste, made from adzuki beans and sugar and available in cans in Asian markets, is a common ingredient in Asian-style dessert dumplings and puddings. They definitely perk up these tasty deep-fried banana treats. **Makes about 30 dim sum servings.**

6 barely ripe bananas, peeled

8 tablespoons sweet red bean paste

1 cup all-purpose flour

2 tablespoons tapioca starch

1 cup water

2 teaspoons baking powder

2 cups peanut or vegetable oil

$^1/_4$ cup sugar

1. Split a banana lengthwise and make a small groove down the middle of both halves. Stuff about 1 tablespoon red bean paste between the 2 halves. Join the halves together and cut into $1^1/_2$-inch (4-cm) sections. Repeat with the remaining bananas and bean paste.

2. Mix the flour and tapioca starch in a large bowl. Gradually add the water and stir until the batter is smooth. Stir in the baking powder. (The consistency of the batter will be rather thick.)

3. Heat the oil in a wok over medium-high heat to 350°F (177°C). In batches of 7 or 8, dip the banana pieces in the batter; add to the hot oil, and deep-fry until golden brown, 6 to 8 minutes. Transfer to paper towels to drain; sprinkle with sugar and serve.

DO AHEAD The fried bananas can be reheated in a 400°F (204°C) oven for 10 minutes.

INDEX